My Dog

Jonathan Allen

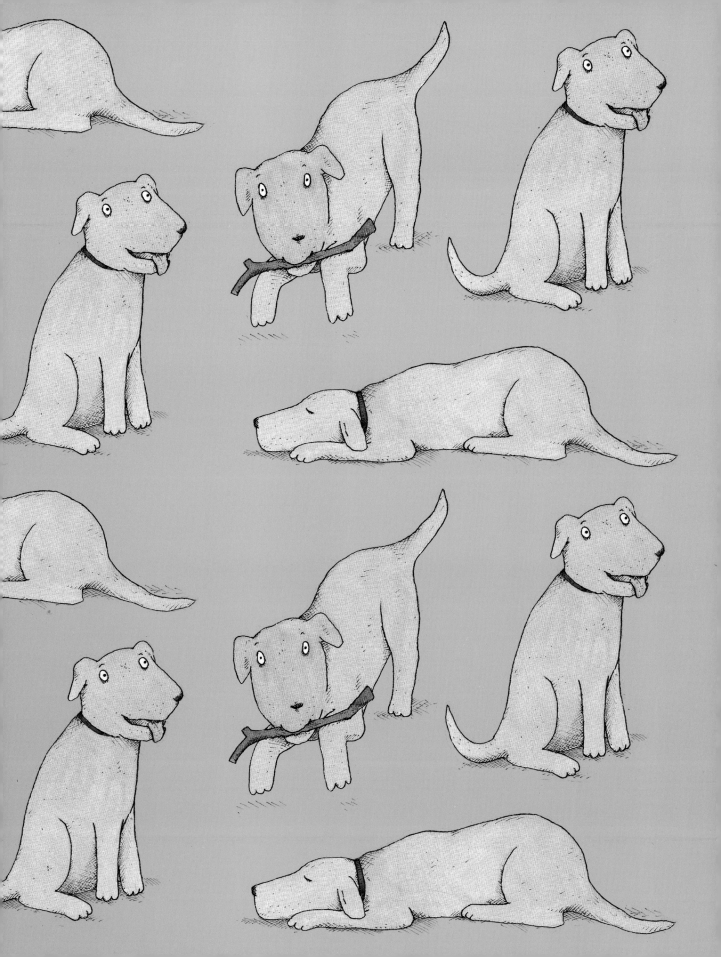

First published in 1987 by Macmillan Children's Books
a division of Macmillan Publishers Limited
20 New Wharf Road, London N1 9RR
Basingstoke and Oxford
Associated companies worldwide
This edition produced 2003 for The Book People Ltd,
Hall Wood Avenue, Haydock, St Helens WA11 9UL.

ISBN 0 333 43814 0 (hardback)
ISBN 0 333 49333 8 (paperback)

Copyright ©1987 Jonathan Allen
Moral rights asserted

1 3 5 7 9 8 6 4 2

A CIP catalogue record for this book is available
from the British Library

Printed in Hong Kong

There are big dogs,

and little dogs,

fat dogs,

and thin dogs.

My dog is a Labrador.

She is very friendly and
jumps up at everyone.

Some people don't like dogs
and get a bit frightened.

When she was a puppy, she used to bite and gnaw things,

so we gave her an old slipper to chew on.

When she was growing up,
I taught her to sit,

to stay,

and to fetch.

Then we played tug-of-war.

When we go out, we always put
her on a lead.
　When we get to the park, I take
it off so she can run around.

She meets other dogs in the park.
They sniff each other.

Sometimes we go out and have to leave her at home. She looks sad and watches us out of the window.

She's so pleased when we come home.
She jumps up, licks my face and wags
her tail.

Sometimes she wags her tail so hard
that she knocks something over.

She's ever so sorry afterwards.

At mealtimes she sits and looks at us hopefully.

We're not allowed to feed her, though.

She has her own food, and my mum and dad let me give it to her.

She barks when she sees people coming to the house.

Once she knows they are friends, she wags her tail.

I like my dog.